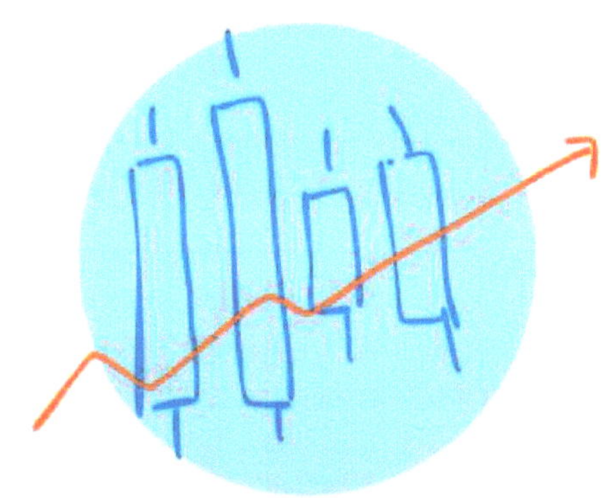

Stalking The Stocks

Simone Kothari

Made with ❤ on the Notion Press Platform

www.notionpress.com

Simone Kothari, a 16-year-old visionary, is driven by her passion for finance, societal and environmental impact, and literature. As a co-founder of *Earth's 911*, a youth-led not-for-profit organization, she is dedicated to creating meaningful change. Simone is also a certified TEDx speaker, a published poet, and a state-level basketball player, demonstrating her versatile talents and leadership. She firmly believes in the transformative power of dialogue and written art. She views financial literacy to be an equally essential skill in today's world. Therefore, she aspires to educate teenagers of the financial boon - The Stock Market through her book 'Stalking the Stocks.'

Preface

The existence of this book.

I am surprised you chose to pick this particular book from the many on the shelf. Given the fact that an alleged 'technical and elderly' concept – finance, has been worded by an unknown teenager, people normally place this book back on the self for it to bathe in dust.

But, I am glad dear friend, that you chose to hold on to both – the book, and your money!

The financial world has always allured me, especially the stock market! Fascinated by the exponential returns of the treasury, I set on my quest of learning more about the market. Little did I know that all the books, and videos I ran through, would be composed with terminologies and concepts that are completely foreign. On top of that, these resources held high expectations from me! An expectation to have some prior understanding of the basics. So basically to know about the market, I needed to already know the market. It felt so unfair, because I, a novice, had no boat to cross the ocean!

Aggrieved, I conceived a thought that today has transcended to be a reality. I aspired to write my own book unearthing the very basics of the stock market, a book that is simple to understand and holds no biasness of background knowledge.

'Stalking the stocks,' a dream fulfilled.

Chapter 1: The beginning of it all

I was in the 5th grade when I heard my parents discussing stocks. I vividly remember a constant word that they used: shares. My forehead wrinkled as I tried to sort through the confusion this concept caused me. My father tried explaining it to me a couple of times, but each time I considered it vague to purchase a product that is intangible, probably imaginary, just something loitering in the air. What's the use of wasting money on it?
Over time, my mother started studying the what-appeared-vague market. Looking at her analyzing the intangibility with utter sincerity, fueled my curiosity. I was ready to come to terms with the 'imaginary product,' even though I was clueless about the entirety of the stock market. All I knew was that a certain bar goes up and down, depending on the direction, its color was decided. Green meant an increase in price while red meant a decrease. So I, in my infinite wisdom, sat beside my mom and bestowed my eternal knowledge onto her.

"My gut tells me this stock is going to have long green bars. Invest!" My gut has remained unheard to this day.

Amongst all this, I recollect a statement I heard from another adult. "Stock market is a gamble," I was appalled. My mother? A gambler? I rushed to her, and asked her "Mom what are you dealing with?" And I was startled yet again, for I got an unreasonable response - a laugh. This soon was justified, as she explained that the stock market is a study of fundamentals and technicalities based on which a decision is formed, however, people who merely follow their gut to prove themselves to others are indirectly gambling. I, for one, buy or sell shares based on my study, thus being a systematic trader. I sighed with relief; my mother's not a gambler.

It was not just the abstract idea of the financial world that allured me, but its ability to nurture wealth and power in young minds was conspicuous too. Remarkable tales of pioneers who earned big being small procured my fondness. Glancing through the Big Bold Words on Google that read; Warren Buffet a billionaire now, started investing at the age of 11, was the catalyst of my aspiration of earning big being small.

The how and when were questions I didn't have answers to myself.

Chapter 2: A knock on the door

As the saying goes, where there is a will, there's a way. Knock, knock! On my doorstep awaits my boat—a school passion project. It is an opportunity to explore the realms of our aspirations and experience living our passions. Without investing another second in the topic, I decided to commence my expedition into the stock market for my passion project.

The thought of being an investor fetched me fantasies of exponential returns on my capital. I found my way to mine money from the stock market's ores! The nights of wide contemplation and ambition engaged frames of newspaper headlines and magazine covers, all highlighting the miraculous success of the young lady—Simone Kothari.

But with the rise of the sun, the bright dreams dimmed for I soon realized that I was yet a novice sailing through this deeper-than-the-Pacific ocean; the Stock Market, and to top it all I didn't have a humongous ship to sail through, all I had in my corner was a little boat.

It was the cacophony of loudly silent questions that gave my ambitions a raincheck. "How does a company get listed in the stock market? How is the stock market beneficial to companies? What does buying a 'share' signify? Who operates the stock market? If somebody marks a loss, to whom is the money disbursed? How do you buy a share? Why will somebody buy a share in a crashing market? And so forth."

I was now cognizant that if I were to prosper, I needed to commence with a strong fundamental knowledge of the market.

So, with the high surges of vocation, I sat on my study table with a device and notebook accompanying me.

Chapter 3: From a Start-up to a Full-grown Business

I soon realized that every thread in the stock market circles back to a company. The company is the primary reason an intangible market exists, where intangible products (the shares) are sold. But the question remains: Why and how does a company's name appear on the stock market?

From the vastness of my deliberations, let's fetch one of my imaginary friends; Timmone. Now I must say, Timmone has a sagacious, quite rare brain. In that landscape of intelligence, a game-changing idea for a start-up conceives! Dedicated, Timmone pitches her idea to investors, convinces her relatives and friends to invest in her vision, and collects seed funding (the initial investment) of 5 crores to afford the bringing up of her start-up, to a full-grown business.

She marks a miraculous success! Her business became part of every conversation in her city. Timmone took pride in her progress, yet she was restless still. "My product can be a boon to every part of this country, not just my city! It shall further prosper through expansion." Through the aid of bank loans and more investors, she increased her retail stores.

"What? How did she convince those investors to invest in her business? Is simply having a way around with our mouths enough to persuade the big pockets? Do they not need certainty of any kind?" Young minds soared with these questions, as they read through the outstanding success of Timmone on various multimedias.

One's oratory skill is not reason enough for an investment of faith and money, multiple financial indicators express the worth of a company. A company's valuation, revenue generation, and sales are among the many indicators.

If you have ever seen glimpses of shark tank pitches on Instagram reels, or for that matter any social media, you must know how the revelation of valuation, revenue generation, and sales can erupt high-magnitude volcanoes of shocks and awe.

Simply put, a valuation is a conglomerate of a company's economic and asset value. It is the sum of a company's monetary, skill, and machine investments.

Revenue generation is the profit a company makes exclusive of all expenses, and sales are the number of goods the company sells. Using such indicators, an investor critically analyzes the scope of the company and deliberates its foreseen scope. Timmone's company's figures stole hearts, persuading the interests of the investors.

Nobody does anything unless they don't get something in return. An investor's financial contribution is exchanged for a stake in the company's ownership, or in a financially recognized phrase; a company's equity. Timmone wisely dissolved 30% of her equity, to get qualified and expert investors on board.

Expert supervision and increased financial capacities enhanced the product's quality. The demand for the product increased exponentially, entailing the need for more production units. However, she could not afford to take more loans from the bank considering the heavy interest they charge, and nor could any investor match the amount she aspired to raise.

This is usually when a company finds its way to the stock market.

Chapter 4: Entering the Gates of the Stock Market

Before we delve deeper into the intriguing triumph of Timmone's start-up, it is important to pay heed to the concept of 'shares.' Imagine that your physical education (PE) coach, yes, that strict and stout figure, whose lips are always wrapped around the whistle, asks you "Hey you, outline a 100 track." Perplexed, you gather guts from the corner of every vein, and ask him "Sir, 100 what?" "Meters, you idiot!" He replies with utter disappointment.

Just like a 'unit' holds immense significance in track and field, it has one in the business world too. Earlier, we spoke about equity, and how it indicates a person's ownership in the company. "20% equity for an investment of 50 lakhs," as the investors say, however, what is the unit that defines the ownership of a person? 20% of what? How is equity measured? Like meters and grams, equity's measuring unit is shares. The company sells the shares at varying prices to the investors. The more shares an investor owns, the larger their stake in the company.

Say for example, your company has issued 100 shares, and each share's price is rs. 10. An investor wants 20% of them in return for their investment, meaning, they shall own 20 shares of your company upon an investment of rs. 200.

It was for the ease of understanding that a number so small was chosen for quantizing the shares, otherwise, the big giants play with 7-8 figures.

Each company's share is worth a different value, depending on the company's product or service's demand. Contingent on the price of one share, the number of shares is proclaimed. For suppose, the valuation of a company is rs. 500, and initially the price of one share is rs.5, this means that the ownership of the company is a constituent of 100 shares. If the company's value increases to rs. 800, the price per share would rise accordingly. There are severals ways of determining the valuation of a company or in other words the value of the company, but the most common and widely used formula of valuation is:

$$Market\ Cap = Share\ Price \times No.of\ shares\ outstanding$$

Coming back to shares, the very initial value of the share, typically in a company's toddler phase is known as the face value. It is the minimum price at which a share can be sold. The face value remains constant, regardless of the progress of the company, unlike the value of the share which is subject to regular fluctuations. The concept of face value is momentous in various actions of the company, ones that we will uncover in the later course of the book.

Now that we understand the concept of shares and face value, let us resume the narrative of Timmone.

Timmone's hassle for funds was later resolved by the company's decision to go public. Meaning, to list itself in the stock market.

So? How will going ‘public’ satisfy the company’s financial needs? Is the company seeking funds from the common people?

Your wrinkled foreheads shall be ironed!

Check For Understanding 1.0

1) A company has 500,000 shares outstanding, and the price of one share is ₹100. What is the market capitalization of the company?

2) A company has a market capitalization of ₹250,000,000, and the share price is ₹500. How many shares are outstanding?

3) A company has 1,000,000 shares outstanding, and each share is priced at ₹1,200. What is the market capitalization?

4) The market capitalization of a company is ₹60,000,000, and the number of shares outstanding is 2,000,000. What is the price of one share?

Chapter 5: The Primary Market

Timmone's company dissolved 25% of its equity and availed it to the public. People like you and me could now buy its 'shares' and purchase our ownership in the company.

The exercise of such power is a result of a process known as IPO (initial public offering). Before the spectacle, the company needed a green signal from SEBI (Securities and Exchange Board of India), the watchdog of the stock market. Succeeding the tedious and rigorous speculations of SEBI, the company finally made it through.

Chasing the approval, the IPO rushed in - the opening gambit for a company's security to go public. The company is currently trading through the primary market, where people like us, buy shares directly with the company.

The investors and traders, however, can only buy through the primary market. They can only sell the shares when the company is listed on the stock exchanges.

Timmone's company announces the issue open date 6 October to 8 October 2024. Her company's 25% of equity quantifies to 2 crore shares. 1.2 crore people are aspiring to purchase equity in her company. Each person's demand for shares varies, some want to purchase 2000, while some want to purchase 200. People place their orders within two days. However, the company has only a limited number of shares publicly available, thus conceiving the possibility that some people are not destined to become her company's shareholders.

The entire process of allotting the shares to respective shareholders is computerized. Based on a random basis, the shares are distributed, evading any sort of bias.

Every buyer that purchases Timmone's company's shares, contributes to the market capitalization of the company. Market capitalization is the product of the number of shares available to the common public and the current price of the share. The money that the company generates during the IPO is utilized by the company in its adverse avenues. The company is not liable to pay the shareholders any interest, and thus, fulfills its financial requirements.

Chapter 6: The Two-Shops

Once Timmone's company's allotment procedure concluded, it transitioned to the **secondary market** and was listed on the two exchanges—NSE and BSE.

An exchange is like a shop, where people find specific goods and services. Think of NSE and BSE as two shops selling shares of Indian companies as their goods. Each of the shops has an overlapping list of goods (i.e. companies), however, the prices at which the same goods are traded differ. It is the customer's preference to choose where they want to buy the goods from.

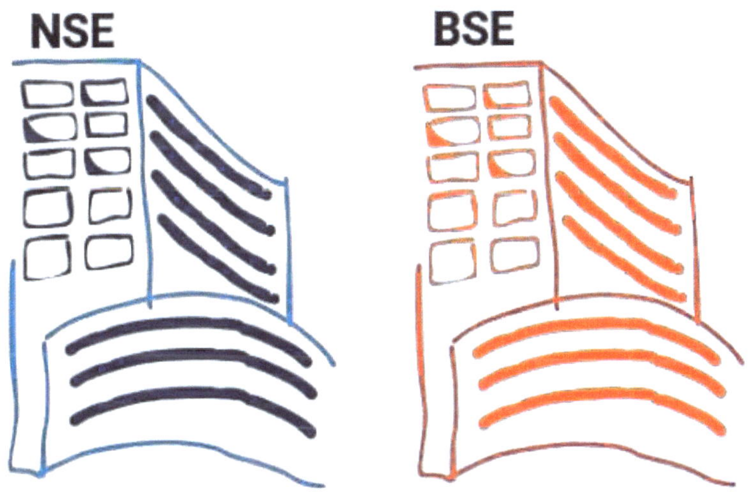

NSE stands for National Stock Exchange, and BSE stands for Bombay Stock Exchange. The two shows are limited to the vicinity of India, other countries have their own exchanges for trading the shares of the companies in their nationality.

Each of these exchanges is a conglomerate of multiple companies ranging from different sectors that include but are not limited to; pharmaceuticals, cosmetics, automobiles, textiles, etc. These fields are like different sections of a grade in school.

Think of yourself to be the principal of the school, and are tasked with analyzing the overall performance of the entire grade 10. As a busy dignitary, you don't have the time and energy to individually monitor the progress, and behavioral comments of each class. Then, how should you determine the grade's progress? Perhaps, selecting a representative from each section, and surveilling their performance is doable, right?

Similarly, these exchanges have indexes - a conglomerate of companies from varying sectors. The indexes give an overview of the trend of the overall market. Each exchange has its individual index. NSE has Nifty and BSE has Sensex. Not any company can become a part of the indices, a company requires certain qualifications in terms of their market capitalization, and more of such figures to enable themselves to become a part of the indices.

Part or not, Timmone's company's share prices have now become visible to all individuals on digital forums such as Trading VIew, Investopedia, Upstox, etc. People can buy and sell shares of her company online, however, this time they will be trading through the secondary market. Meaning, that there is no more a direct relationship between her company and a trader; the exchanges are now the middlemen between the two.

Check For Understanding 2.0

Identify which image represents which market:

____________________ ____________________

Chapter 7: Bulls and Bears

Thus far, we know how Timmone's company cleared the primary market and entered the secondary market, where its shares can be traded through either of the exchanges. However, if you have ever had the tiniest of a glance at applications that broadcast the live charts of a company, you must have noticed that the prices of the shares are constantly fluctuating, they're quite restless. The first question that came running to me as I first glimpsed at the prices' versatile nature was - WHY? Why do the prices keep changing, who changes it?

To my surprise, the answer lay in the concept that I learned in grade 4 - supply and demand! Let me break it down for you.

After the listing of Timmone's company in the exchanges, multiple people invested their faith in her company, not just figuratively but literally too - with their money. On the other hand, certain people who were already share-owners of her company through the IPO, seeked to sell their shares and invest their money elsewhere.
Now, like any conventional economic activity - a buyer buys from a seller who sells the product that they intend to buy. They both negotiate a price as per their convenience, and buy and sell shares respectively, an exact transaction takes place in the stock market.

This might sound unrealistic, but when there are millions of people waiting to exit and enter the market, each buyer and each seller find a seller, and a buyer respectively, to complement their needs.

The only difference between a conventional economic transaction and a transaction in the stock market is that the buyer and seller are unaware of who they are trading the shares with. Meaning, the buyer has no clue of the person who is willing to fulfill their demands. It is so because the exchanges interfere, and facilitate the process to complete with anonymity.

Contingent on the demand and the supply of the shares of Timmone's company, her share price fluctuates. If there are more buyers in the market than the sellers, then they drive the market price up. Likewise, if there are more sellers in the market than buyers, then they drive the prices down.

Let us utilize this moment to enter a zoo. Where there are multiple animals. Although, your eyes are specifically focused on the bull. Because the bull was waging an attack on the other bull. And you, being a typical teenager, obviously love drama! You then noticed how the bull charged with its horn thrusting upwards, and pushed the other bull with all its strength.
After 5 minutes or so, you grew tired of the bullfight. Neither of the fighters was able to defeat the other. So, you went on your way, exploring the zoo.

Hardly a few seconds passed until you stopped again. This time, it was the bears who became a source of your entertainment. The bears, like the bulls, indulged in a fight. But, unlike the bulls, they fought by swiping their paws downward. “Bizzare.” You murmured. Between the fight, and your distracted attention, a memory card projected itself in your mind. Yes, the movement of the prices in the stock market.

Similar to the bull, the prices rush up (positive), and similar to a bear they crash down (negative). This resemblance entitled the buyer to be 'Bulls' and the sellers to be 'Bears.' The one that fights stronger influences the direction of the prices (i.e. whether it will increase or decrease).
This is another reason you may quite often hear the phrases 'Bullish market' and 'Bearish market,' the phrase simply signifies the market trends. Bullish market indicates an uptrend, while bearish market indicates a downtrend.

The trends are influenced by the current affairs of the world, by the decisions of the company, and by many more factors. If Timmone's company announces that they will soon be starting with a new product's manufacturing line, it showcases that her company is prospering. The release of the new newspaper headlines are likely to influence the buyers to buy shares. The more the bears, the stronger the bullish trend. Likewise, if the world hears that the CEO of Timmone's company is resigning, the people will interpret that the company's management is vulnerable – they might lose faith in the company, and sell the shares. Spearheading a bearish trend.

The stock market is synonymous to an ecosystem. It has its own food chain, where the interconnectedness of various stakeholders impacts the prices of the shares of a company.

Check For Understanding 3.0

Identify which diagram represents which trend of the market:

____

____

Chapter 8: Trading VS Investing

Quite often people use these two terms 'trading' and 'investing' interchangeably, but these two words are two distinct actions with two distinct objectives.

Investing is a testament of patience. Investors generally buy shares and hold them for more than a year. While traders buy and sell shares within a shorter time frame – sometimes on the same day, sometimes the same week, and sometimes the same month, depending on their analysis.

You can be both. A trader and an investor together. For instance, you want to be financially secured, but also want to generate a monthly and quarterly income from the stock market. Dedicated, you surfed through multiple companies and found Timmone's business idea and growth captivating. In turn to your captivation, you purchased 5000 shares of her company. You had no intention of selling the shares anytime soon, because, as per your study of the company, you projected incredulous returns in the coming 5 years. So you chose to hold on.

Uh, you may have secured your 5-years-down-the-line future, but, how were you to survive financially in the present?

In such cases, people resort to trading. They buy shares with the intention of selling it in the near future, so that they can generate short-term incomes.

An investor:

- Aspires to gradually gain returns on their investment
- Disregards the bearish trends of the market, for they believe the market will rebound in the longer-term
- Usually resorts to the stock market to have a parallel income stream alongside their business
- Who is unaware of the market, its behavior, and its principles, reaches out to Domestic Asset Management Companies (AMC) – mutual fund companies, that invest on their behalf, in exchange of the transaction fee they charge
- Passive investors buy and forget the shares until a few years later. They don't regularly monitor the progress of the share.
- Active investors on the other hand, might choose to add or subtract their shareholdings based on the company's performance.

A trader:

- Deals with a riskier financial environment. As they aim to generate similar profit percentages of long-term holding, within a shorter time frame.
- Regularly tracks the company's performance, and makes decisions accordingly.
- Can ***short sell***, unlike an investor.

The charactics of the two positions are what distinguishes them. Mainly based on the time horizon, but also with the privileges associated with them.

Check For Understanding 4.0

Categorize the following descriptions under 'investor' or 'trader'

1. Long-term, steady approach to growing wealth, may not actively track performance. (______________)
2. Believes the market will recover in the long-term despite short-term downturns. (______________)
3. Engages in higher-risk trading, aiming to make profits in a short time. (______________)
4. Often turns to mutual funds or AMCs for professional investment management. (______________)
5. Buys shares with the intention of holding them for a long time, not checking on them regularly. (______________)
6. Actively tracks stock performance and frequently buys and sells based on market trends. (______________)
7. Engages in short selling, betting that stock prices will decrease. (______________)

Chapter 9: "Short selling?"

The use of this phrase 'shot selling' most probably invited raised eyebrows and wrinkled foreheads. Before uncovering this process, let us have a walk down a conventional process of buying a share.

You recently won a lottery of rs. 25000. Unlike a spoiled teenager, you chose to invest this money in the stock market, rather than spending it all on some bougie materialistic desires.

Manifesting for profits, you yearned for becoming a shareholder of Timmone's company. Craving for profits, you were waiting for the right time to enter the market. You were aware that you can only mark a profit if the market follows a bullish trend, common sense, right? Because, if the bulls overpower the bears, the price of the shares will drive up, and that way you'll be able to sell the shares at a higher price then what you bought it at.

This procedure of buying low and selling high is known as 'long position' where you expect the price of the share to increase.

But, your ambitions are soon challenged by the disclosure of Timmone's company's annual earning report. The report, to your disappointment, was a poor one. As a repercussion, the company's stock prices de-escalated hastily, vandalizing the unreal reality you were daydreaming of. Looking at the negative aura of the company's chart, you wondered —
"Is there no way to make profits in the bearish market?"

"Short-selling" The universe replied.

It is the UNO reverse card of 'long position' – you first sell the shares at a higher price, and later buy the shares at a lower price, as the market descends and throughout the trade you expect the market to fall.

Huh? How can you sell something that you don't own? Sounds absurd, right? But short term trading avails this benefit.

Let us understand the 'how' of short selling in a brief.

Since you wanted to generate profits even out of the crashing market of Timmone's company, you resorted to 'short selling.' Amidst which, you first sold the shares at a higher price. The amount you sold the shares at will be credited (added) in your account. But, as previously mentioned, you need to have a product (i.e share) to sell it to others, so where do you get the product from? The brokers.

The ***brokers*** lend you shares from their inventory. So technically you are actually selling a product but one that was loaned to you by your broker.

Done. You asked your ***broker*** to short sell shares in Timmone's company. Now that you had already sold the product, you waited to buy the shares back.
And so, every vein in your body manifests for the prices to go further down, so that you buy the shares at the cheapest rate possible and

enjoy wholesome returns. Because, the higher you sell, and the lower you buy, the wealthier you become.

To close the short sale, you must buy back the same number of shares that you sold. This process is known as '**closing.**' Once you buy those shares back, you must return them to your ***broker***, and become debt free.

Mind you though, if the market does not favour your wishes, and instead, the bulls take over. Then my friend, you will still have to cover your position, and the irony – you will have to bear a loss in a bullish market.

Check For Understanding 5.0

Tick the correct option.

1. What is a "long position" in the stock market?

a) Selling shares at a lower price to profit when the price goes up.

b) Buying shares with the expectation that the price will increase.

c) Borrowing shares from a broker to sell them at a higher price.

d) Selling shares at a higher price and buying them back at a lower price.

2. What is the main goal of short selling?

a) To buy shares at a low price and sell them at a higher price.

b) To profit from the price increase of a stock.

c) To profit from the price decrease of a stock.

d) To buy shares and hold them indefinitely.

3. How does short selling differ from buying and holding stocks?

a) In short selling, you sell shares before you own them.

b) In buying and holding, you expect the price to go down.

c) In short selling, you wait for the price to go up.

d) Buying and holding is risk-free, while short selling has no risk.

4. Who lends the shares to the short seller in the stock market?

a) The stock exchange.

b) The company whose shares are being traded.

c) Brokers or stock market applications.

d) Other investors.

5. What happens when you "close" a short sale?

a) You buy back the shares you sold and return them to the broker.

b) You hold onto the shares indefinitely.

c) You sell the shares again at a higher price.

d) You transfer the shares to another broker.

6. What could happen if the stock price increases after you short sell?

a) You make a profit.

b) You lose money and have to buy back the shares at a higher price.

c) The broker buys the shares back for you.

d) You become debt-free.

7. Why is short selling referred to as the "UNO reverse card" of long positions?

a) It allows you to profit from the market going up.

b) It allows you to profit from a market decline, opposite of the usual buying method.

c) It involves buying shares before selling them.

d) It is the safest way to invest.

8. Which of the following is true about short selling?

a) The short seller buys shares and holds them to sell later.

b) The short seller profits when the stock price increases.

c) The short seller borrows shares from a broker to sell them at a high price.

d) The short seller keeps the borrowed shares indefinitely.

Chapter 10: 'Broker' who?

Have you ever wanted to invest in the stock market but felt like it was a world reserved for the experts? What if I told you there's a middleman who makes it all possible?

"Brokers." This is your one stop solution.

In the previous chapter, it was implicitly mentioned that for short selling, a trader needs to be associated with either a broker, or a stock market application. *But who and what is a broker?*

Summer vacations are around the corner, and I have plans for Thailand. Sitting by the beach, bathing in the yellows, and inhaling the beauty of nature. Ugh, but who will undergo the process of looking for hotels, planning the itinerary. This is a story for most of us.

"Travel Agents." Yeah, I heard you.

Travel agents are professionals that help people like us to book our hotels, plan our itinerary, book our air fares, basically everything that involves the word 'booking' is done by them. They serve as mediators between the country and us.

Just like them, we have brokers. The mediators of the stock market. A broker is like the travel agent for your investments. But instead of booking flights and hotels, they help you buy and sell stocks.

They are recognized by exchanges, and are appropriately certified with a license granted by our watchdog - SEBI (Securities and Exchange Board of India). There are multiple brokers in India, out of which you can choose the one that you want to open your client account with. Brokers ensure that all the trades that you deliberate on making, comply with the guidelines of SEBI.

At one point of time, you were expected to ring the broker everytime you wanted to buy or sell a share. That could be time-consuming and frustrating. But with the rise of technology, platforms from accredited banks and companies like Kotak, Upstox, and Grow now allow you to trade stocks with just a swipe of your finger. This shift allows you to timely buy and sell shares, maximizing profits and minimizing losses.

"Wow, these days it is rare to find people who guide you for free. A tribute to these brok--"

Hold on, hold on. Money has become synonymous to happiness, why would anyone provide a service, especially as crucial a service as this, for free? Brokerage. Brokerage is what the brokers charge the clients with.

Every share that you buy or sell is accompanied by a percentage that you're supposed to pay your broker with. Some brokers charge an annual fee, while some charge a fixed percentage for every transaction you make.

To seize, just like a travel agent trades money with saving your time and stress on vacation planning, a broker helps you navigate the complexities of the stock market, giving you the tools you need to make informed investment decisions and manage your portfolio, charging you with brokerage in exchange.

Chapter 11: Technicals and fundamentals

Oof, I believe that at this point it is safe to assume that you are well versed with the concept of buying and selling a share, both in a prosperous, and an impoverishing market. With the current knowledge database, you might consider yourself ready to enter the battlefield and return home victorious.

But ready, you are not.

You know how some people—especially those insightful aunties—can look at you and seemingly read your soul with one glance, instantly creating an entire biography in their mind? Well, the stock market works in a similar way. It's all about judgment.

When it comes to evaluating the movement of share prices, there are two primary methods: fundamental analysis and technical analysis.

Similarly, the stock market is a game of judgement too. There are two ways of judging the movement of the share prices of companies; fundamental and technical analysis.

Fundamental analysis looks at the factors that influence a company's stock price. This includes a deep dive into financial reports, economic conditions, corporate decisions, and qualitative elements behind the company's operations. Essentially, it focuses on understanding the "why" behind a stock's movement—how the company's performance, its management, and market conditions affect its value.

On the other hand, technical analysis revolves around the stock price itself. Rather than investigating the reasons behind the price movement, it focuses on patterns in the price data. Traders who use technical analysis study price charts, identify trends, and rely on specific indicators—like candlestick patterns or moving averages—to predict future price movements. It generalizes the patterns and the indicators into a system, and trades shares using that system.

"Eh, what is a system?"

System simply put, is like a rule that traders follow. The rule dictates them about when to enter the market, when to exit the market, and what **stop loss** to put. After extensively reading the market, or registering in certain courses, people become cognizant of such systems. A system's effectiveness is not limited to 'trading' but is applicable to 'investing' too.

Both methods—fundamental and technical analysis—have their own strengths and weaknesses. To truly succeed in the stock market, it's important to understand both approaches. Neither is perfect, but each offers valuable insights that can guide your investment decisions.

Check For Understanding 6.0

Fill in the blanks

1. Fundamental analysis considers factors such as economic conditions, corporate decisions, and financial reports, which contribute to understanding the ___________behind a stock's price.

2. Technical analysis ignores the underlying factors influencing a company's stock price and focuses solely on the _________ data, such as chart patterns and price movements.

3. A trader who uses fundamental analysis typically focuses on the company's _________, like profit margins, leadership decisions, and market share, to gauge the stock's long-term potential.

4. While ___________ **analysis** is often used for long-term investing, _________ **analysis** is typically favored by those interested in short-term trading or speculation.

5. A system used by traders helps them make objective decisions about when to _________ or exit the market, reducing emotional biases in trading.

Chapter 12: Candlestick breakdown

If you hear somebody say the word 'stock market' or if you read the word aloud, then what is the first image that pops in your mind?

The 12-year-old me always considered the above attached image to be the definition of the market. Little did I know that this image only encapsulates the 'technical' part of the market.

I was fascinated by the constant movement of the prices, and how it held the power to change the color of the candle. When I made an effort to go beyond my fascination, I returned with my brows furrowed. My one hand reached up to tug at a loose strand of hair, while my other hovered over the mouse, unmoving. My eyes narrowed, blinking rapidly, trying to make sense of the candles.
Allow me to zoom in the candle, and paint my confusion to you.

At which part of the candle is the closing price decided?

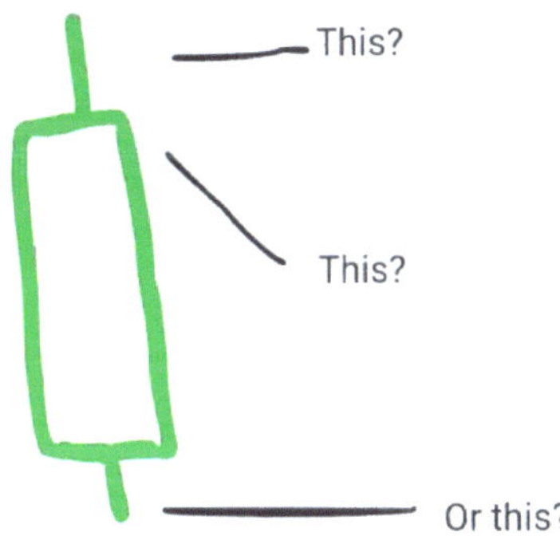

It was after this confusion that I realized the significance of the candles. Each part of the candle represents a price, and each of these prices hold distinct meanings. You might have heard a very commonly used abbreviation in the stock market 'OHLC,' this is what the different parts express.

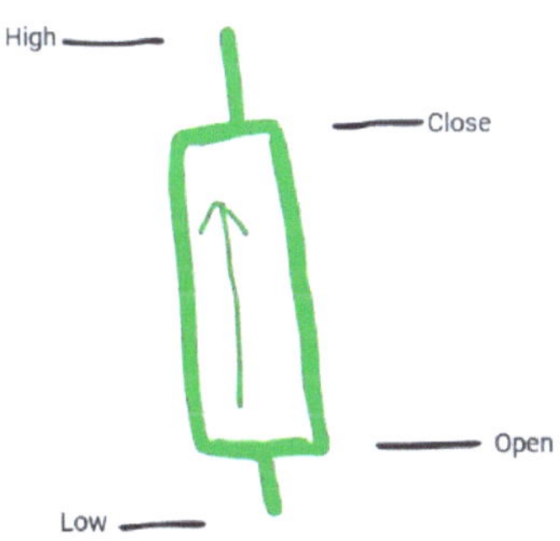

O stands for the open, H stands for high, L stands for low and C stands for close. The points have been annotated in the diagram as well. In a bullish candle, the upper side of the rectangle determines the price at which the candle stops moving at. While the downside of the rectangle signifies the price at which the candle opened at. 'High' means the highest price at which the share was traded at, conversely low means the lowest price at which the share was traded at.

Things change when the color of the candles changes to red -- a bearish candle.

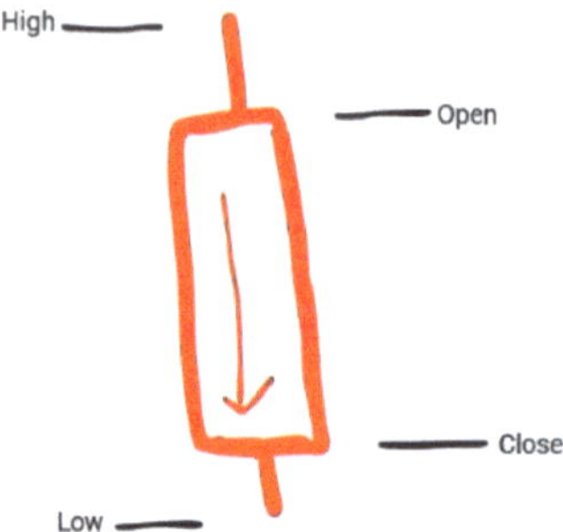

The open and close parts have swapped their places. But, why?

A bearish candle turns red, because the share is being traded at a lower price then what it was opened at. Meaning, if a share opens at rs. 20 today, and by the end of the day, the last price it was traded at is rs. 18, then the candle that appears will be red in color. This is why a bearish candle has exchanged parts determining the opening and closing price.

You might wonder what those sticks and the rectangle are known for, for everything we see has certain labels associated with them, and obviously the candles are no exception. Attached on the right is a diagram of a candle. The annotated parts are known as the same for both a bullish and a bearish candle.

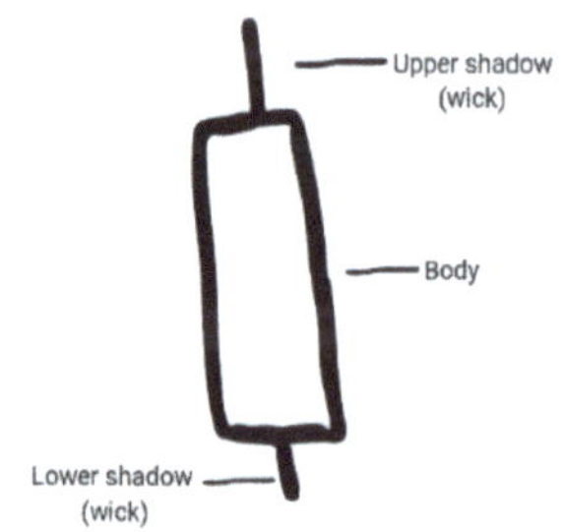

As soon as I sought answers for one question, my greedy mind conceived another. "Why do new candles keep appearing next to each other? Why does a new candle appear?"

This image is 'why' a new candle appears. The image showcases different time intervals; 1 day, 5 days (i.e. 1 week), 1 month, 3 months, 6 months and so on and so forth. After the end of every time interval, a new candle is formed. So if you were to check a stock's monthly progress, you would be referring to the monthly chart. Based on these time intervals, traders scrutinize different systems, and trade using those.

Chapter 13: Corporate actions

For quite some time we haven't spoken about Timmone's company, right? Let's bring her onboard again!

Timmone's company is continuing to excel, touch wood. And the board of directors of her company want to reward their shareholders for showcasing trust in them through their money. Generally, there are three ways through which companies generally reward their shareholders or show them that they are prospering. Way 1 - Bonus shares, Way 2 - Stock Split, Way 3 - Dividends.

Bonus shares:

As the phrase suggests itself, bonus shares are a 'bonus' to existing shareholders. For instance, you hold 50 shares in Timmone's company, and the current share price is rs. 100. Owing to the company's success, they announce that they will be giving bonus shares to every shareholder in the ratio 1:1, meaning for every share that you hold, you will receive one more share for free.

So, after the bonus shares have been allotted to you, you will have a total of 100 shares. The stock price of the share will decrease in the same ratio, thus, your shares will now be tradeable at rs. 50.

Stock split:

Very similar to bonus shares, a stock split is usually announced when a company wants to make their shares more affordable. Commonly, the prices of shares of certain companies hike to such an extent that it becomes difficult for traders and investors to put their money in motion. That is when a company declares the splitting of stocks.

Assuming that a company is currently trading at rs. 1500, and it decides to split every share in the ratio of 4:1, then for every 1 share that a shareholder owns, they will have 4 more. If you have 50 shares, then after the split, you will have 200 shares. The only difference between a stock split and bonus shares is that the face value decreases in the same ratio as a stock split, while it remains unchanged during bonus shares.

Dividend:
A dividend however, is a reward that a company gives without changing the number of shares that a shareholder owns. Dividends usually go like 'Dividend of rs. 10 on every share that you hold,' meaning you earn rs. 10 on every share. The more shares in your possession, the richer you become.

If a company gives dividends this year, it may choose to not give them the coming year, depending on its growth. There are also companies like Apple and Google that choose not to give dividends regardless of their prosperous reports. It is so because they believe the same amount can be used to reinvest in the company for its growth, and down the line all shareholders will benefit from a more developed setup of the companies.

These corporate actions have made many billionaires. People who hold large quantities of shares have become overnight money minters.

Chapter 14: The End

As this book comes to a close, take a moment to reflect on all the concepts you've encountered within these pages. Each idea, strategy, and piece of advice has been carefully simplified to help you gain a foundational understanding of the stock market. However, remember this: the stock market is not a small pond, but a vast, unpredictable ocean. And while you've taken your first sip, the journey ahead is far from over.

In the world of investing and trading, there will always be more to explore, more to learn, and new challenges to face. What you've learned here is just the beginning—like a map to guide you through the tides of the financial world. The real mastery comes with experience, with observing the market, adapting your strategies, and learning from both successes and failures.

As you venture forward, don't rush to dive into deep waters just yet. Instead, take your time. With every decision, with every trade, you will refine your skills and expand your understanding. Be patient with yourself, stay curious, and remember that no one becomes an expert overnight. The market will teach you as much as you are willing to learn, and the journey will be as rewarding as the destination itself.

So, take the knowledge you've gained, but keep in mind that this is just the start. The ocean is vast, and you have only just begun to chart its waters. Keep sailing, keep learning, and soon you'll find yourself navigating with confidence.

Answer Key

Check For understanding 1.0

1) Market Cap = 100 × 500,000 = ₹50,000,000
2) No. of Shares Outstanding = $\frac{Market\ capitalization}{Share\ price}$

   $\frac{250{,}000{,}000}{500}$ = 500, 000
3) Market Cap = 1,200 × 1,000,000 = ₹1,200,000,000
4) Share price = $\frac{Market\ capitalization}{No.of\ shares\ outstanding}$

   $\frac{60{,}000{,}000}{2{,}000{,}000}$ = ₹30

Check For understanding 2.0

a) Primary Market b) Secondary Market

Check For understanding 3.0

a) Bullish trend OR uptrend b) Bearish trend OR downtrend

Check For understanding 4.0

1. Investor 2. Investor 3. Trader 4. Investor 5. Investor 6. Trader 7. Trader

Check For understanding 5.0

1. **b)** Buying shares with the expectation that the price will increase.
2. **c)** To profit from the price decrease of a stock.
3. **a)** In short selling, you sell shares before you own them.
4. **c)** Brokers or stock market applications.

5. **a)** You buy back the shares you sold and return them to the broker.
6. **b)** You lose money and have to buy back the shares at a higher price.
7. **b)** It allows you to profit from a market decline, opposite of the usual buying method.
8. **c)** The short seller borrows shares from a broker to sell them at a high price.

Check For understanding 6.0

1. Why
2. Price
3. Fundamental
4. Fundamental analysis; Technical analysis
5. Enter

www.ingramcontent.com/pod-product-compliance
Lightning Source LLC
LaVergne TN
LVHW021345160826
845679LV00008B/1480

* 9 7 9 8 8 9 6 9 9 0 0 1 7 *